Circe's Bicycle

Circe's Bicycle

Tara Campbell

Lit Fest Press

ISBN: 978-1-943170-25-8

Cover and Interior Design: Jane L. Carman

Published by: Lit Fest Press, Carman, 688 Knox Road 900 North,
Gilson, Illinois 61436

Lit Fest Press

Outside the box

Tradition

&

Transition

Monkey Roast

"That's not the way you cut monkey roast," said mother.

I looked up, knife and fork poised above the turkey.

She gestured with knotted fingers. "You start at the tail."

I moved to the end of the bird.

"Did you save the balls for the gravy, dear?"

"Happy Thanksgiving, Mom," I lied.

Stardust

Little sister, all stardust and unicorns, pink and glitter and sticky hands, constantly following him around. How could he know she would grow up and shake out her pigtails, inhale a soft new glitter, follow the unicorns instead? She's lost; he can only look up and see her in stardust.

Freedom Bras

This morning I woke up and looked at my bras
washed yesterday, hung to dry
lined up like the heads of my enemies
bras of a certain age
like the ones my mother wore
when I wondered why they looked like tanks.

Look who's driving tanks now.
They're softer and smaller, but still a far cry
from the tiny, sleek models I zipped around in
after ditching my sister's scratchy hand-me-downs
training bras, because discomfort needs practice.

How many times, sneaking out the door to play
hand on the doorknob,
did my shoulders hunch at my mother's voice:
Put on a bra
hitch on that ancient, lace-strewn itch-monkey
that's the cost of admission to the world, my dear,
the fee for growing up,
that's the price of freedom.

Tara Campbell

When Peanut Butter Baby Ruled the World

It began with the dreaming mothers.

No one ever found out why
but one by one
the new babies came into the world

> Pickle Baby
> Ice Cream Baby
> Crispy Tofu Baby

The first births were recorded
by nurses with trembling hands.
Others came

> Chocolate Baby
> Nutella Baby
> Marshmallow Baby

The phenomenon had no ground zero, no borders.
Doctors around the world compared notes

> Cassava Baby
> Chickpea Baby
> Spicy Squid Baby

and searched for a cure,
meanwhile pleading with mothers to maintain their health.

The mothers tried

> Asparagus Baby
> Broccoli Baby
> Peanut Butter Baby

But they had needs

> Bacon Baby
> Rum Baby
> Maraschino Cherry Baby
> Tiny Umbrella Baby

They couldn't control their dreams...

> Vodka Baby
> Wine Baby
> Gin & Tonic Baby
> Highball Baby

...of all the things they couldn't have

> Marlboro Baby
> Virginia Slims Baby
> Raw Cookie Dough Baby
> Unpasteurized Milk Baby

The doctors kept waking them up to feed them applesauce and admonishment, but they kept on dreaming...

> Imported Soft Cheese Baby
> Beef Tartare Baby
> Sushi Baby
> Swordfish Baby
> Just About Any Goddamn Fish Baby

...until finally the mothers said, "Enough!
> We still love Pickle Baby
> and Crispy Tofu Baby
> and Peanut Butter Baby

and Highball Baby
and yes, even Just About Any Goddamn Fish Baby is okay.
They're all our babies."

And then they dreamed whatever they wanted.

And by the time Peanut Butter Baby grew up and ruled the world
there were even more kinds of babies, like

Equal Pay Baby
No More Street Harassment Baby
Corporate Leadership Equity Baby
Elimination of Female Genital Mutilation Baby

and

Respect Your Elders Baby,
who eventually had
To Hell With Plastic Surgery Baby

and

Male Pregnancy Baby,
who gave immediate birth to
Right to Choose Baby
and her twin
Self-Determination Baby

And when Self-Determination Baby usurped the throne
her first and last order
before abolishing the position of Ruler of the World
was to tell the mothers to dream
and keep on dreaming.

AND-IF-I

dream this
pinprick essence
core-bright
blue

sense this

tight white ball,

this furnace fierce,

think this ball expanding,

magma flow, see this saffron pulp

gold molten slush, feel this liquid warmth

this lapping heat, hold this rippling thinness,

wrinkling sheet – then I crack   this hueless shell

such brittle pains   crush these shards of greatness

browning   grains   and   loose   this

blackened   powder   no

remains.

Spin Art

Hear the thud of your body against the window.
    Feel, for an instant, the cool, smooth glass on your
        cheek. Hear the tinkle as it shatters. Feel the shards
            cut a million slits in your skin. Don't hear anyone
                scream—they haven't had time yet. Feel the
                    wind blowing blood across your
                      skin like straw-and-ink
                        art, like Spin Art, only
                          you're not spinning
                            really, you're

                                    only

                                      going

                                        in

                                          one

                                            direction

Where the Words Go

Sometimes her words simply fell away unnoticed, like pearls through a careless queen's fingers. But one was as good as the other, and she had too many to miss a few. When she came across them again, glinting in the shag carpet her children kept telling her to upgrade, she would dig them up from the dusty strands, blow off the dirt—as good as new.

Sometimes they dropped like breadcrumbs she never meant to leave behind. She thought they were in her mouth, but they vanished from her tongue, leaving only a flavor she couldn't quite name. But almost-right sufficed.

Soon enough, the words were kittens hiding under couches. Someone younger would pull them out and utter them into her lap, where they settled and purred. Teeth clenched behind a smile, she squeezed her knees together so the words wouldn't slip out again.

Why wouldn't they stay in her lap, her mouth, her hands? Sometimes they rolled off her palms and hid for days. She'd wait until after dark, go out with a flashlight and find them glittering in the cracks of sidewalks, tumbling down dark alleys, purring in other people's lawns. She had to approach them sideways, half looking, or they would scatter.

Often now, they flicker at the edges of her vision, flitting to a new periphery every time she moves her head. She sees the tree limbs shivering, but she can't see the words through the leaves. How did they get up there?

Why won't the words stay in her head? Do they know something she doesn't?

Is there something dangerous there?

Perhaps she'll start collecting empty boxes. She'll label them WORDS and stick them in the attic and tell herself that's where the words go when they leave her. They'll all be up there, next to her light-up rooftop Santa, her deceased husband's service records and her children's basketball and spelling bee trophies. She'll have the foresight to put packing peanuts in the boxes, so if she ever goes up and shakes them, she'll hear something rattle. She'll know that the words are still there, waiting for her, whenever she wants them.

But with time, as more words escape her, it will be more difficult for her to follow them into the attic. Her shoulder will protest when she reaches for the ladder; her knees will groan on the steps. Her children, when they visit, will give her the words she's looking for. She'll worry about wasting theirs—she always loses them again—and insist they go up and get some of hers. But her children will tell her they've thrown out their backs, or the attic is too dusty, or they'll climb up there for the words next time, but for the meantime, they'll just give her some of theirs. They'll say they don't mind if she misplaces them, they have more where those came from.

Besides, they'll tell her, you gave them to us in the first place.

And they'll have so many words, they'll never miss a few.

Captain John's Passage

"You sure about this?" asked the cook, wiping a tattered red handkerchief across his brow.

Captain John squinted against the sun and scratched at his scraggly, pecan-colored beard. "Who in blazes knows, Cookie?" He prodded the unmoving figure on the sand with his boot. "But aye, I reckon we should tie him up."

Cookie frowned. "Fine, soon's you show me how to tie up a piece of goo."

Captain John stared at the globular creature sprawled out at their feet. He hadn't been trained to handle anything like this. One minute he and his crew were battling a storm at sea, the next minute he and Cookie were stuck in some desert. Then this impossible purple alien comes out of nowhere.

"Lemme think," he said, looking around the arid expanse they'd thought was a lake. His tongue played at the grains of sand on the back of his teeth. If there were any stones around, he'd put them in his mouth and suck on them. That's what he'd always heard you did for thirst, anyway. Not that he, as a sea captain, ever thought he'd be stranded in the desert.

"Best hurry that thinkin' up," said Cookie. "What if there's more like him comin'?" He jerked his head toward the blob on the sand.

Captain John looked down at the creature and pulled at his beard. "Somethin' tells me his army ain't nowhere 'round here." He wasn't sure what made him think that. Maybe it was how the creature had quivered when it approached—'course, how else would a gelatinous thing like that look when it moved?

"Dunno Cap. If there's more of 'em around, they'll be lookin' for water just like this one. Just like us."

The captain crouched over the purple blot on the sand and sniffed. It smelled kind of vinegary, with a whiff of boiled potatoes to boot. He stood and crossed his arms. There was something about the way it came at them, at their flasks to be exact, like it didn't want to touch anything but their water. It had no way of knowing the flasks had been empty for days, but it seemed to know what they were supposed to hold. If that was the case, if this thing knew more about them than they about it—dangerous state of affairs, this.

"Captain, look!"

A stately, sand-faring ship approached, white sails billowing, parting mustard-colored dunes with its prow. The craft shushed to a halt before them. A railing creaked open; a gangplank descended over the lip of the deck, guided by unseen hands.

The two men looked at each other, then back up at their best chance for survival.

"What should we do with him?" asked Cookie.

Captain John stared at the purple blob, hard. The creature lay there, all shriveled and gritty, like the captain's own tongue had flopped onto the sand and tried to crawl away for help.

Cookie's breath whistled in and out through his nostrils.

Still, thought the captain, there was something sad in the way the creature had pulled away from his fists, twisted away from his kicking boot. Now, puckered and covered in sand, it looked like a helpless jellyfish washed ashore.

Cookie's breath whistled in, whistled out.

Captain John clenched his teeth, picked up the alien and slung it over his shoulder.

Cookie smiled wide.

Captain John grunted and started up the gangplank. Vinegar smell like to knock him out, but the thing wasn't as slimy as he thought it'd be. Probably too dried out by now. Halfway up, he turned back to see why the cook's boots weren't clomping up the plank behind him.

Cookie stood on the sand, not moving, but not completely still either. Fuzzy.

Captain John shook his head and squeezed his eyes shut, wishing he could let go of his load to rub them. The cook was still out of focus when he opened his eyes again.

"Cookie, come on," he called out, hefting the alien's weight on his shoulder. "You're wastin' daylight."

The cook's form wavered and shifted. As Captain John looked on, Cookie's body fragmented and blew away in the wind.

"Don't worry," said Cookie's voice. "You won't be needin' me anymore. You passed."

Light swelled within the ship. Captain John turned slowly around to face the enveloping glow.

Circe's Bicycle

The moth came one night in October. Mallory still isn't sure where it came from, not that it matters anymore.

That night she awoke to a fluttering in her ear. Her fingertips brushed against a tumble of wings and she jolted awake. The streetlamp shining through the window illuminated a tiny blur of grey over her bed. The moth (which had been right next to her ear, she thought with a shudder) stumbled through the air, evidently knocked out of its path by her waving hand, and landed on the hill of her husband's knee under the blankets.

She worried about the wool suits in the closet.

Her husband snored.

Out the window you go, she thought (to the moth, not her husband), and inched her legs toward the edge of the mattress. The moth flitted back into the air. She slid out of bed and slipped into her fuzzy pink house shoes, which were a little goofy, but she wore them because her daughter Amy had picked them out.

Mallory stepped to the window and opened it, then turned to look for the moth. It fumbled above the bed, fat and woolly, flashing grey to white to grey again as it lurched across the grid of lamplight shining through the windowpane. She crossed to the bed and swatted at the hairy insect, not wanting to actually make contact. She waved currents of air in its direction, trying to sweep the grape-sized menace out the window.

The cold floor chilled her feet through her slippers. The soles were getting thin after a few years, but she wouldn't throw them out. They were the last present she would ever get from her daughter. The car had struck Amy on her bike a month after Mother's Day. She was almost seven.

Mallory's husband snored on.

She pursed her lips. None of their battles were shared. She was still trapped in the wreckage of Amy's bicycle. It had pink tassels and a unicorn painted on the seat. She and her husband had widened their eyes at each other when their daughter had picked it out, silently asking each other, *So girlie; where did she get that from?* Mallory still pushed and bled against twisted metal in her sleep. Her husband slept the night through.

Mallory thought it was just her imagination when the moth grew to the size of an egg. She could almost hear the thrum of its wings from across the room. But those could only be the tricks of a tired, frustrated mind, like those nights after the funeral she thought she heard her daughter's footsteps between her husband's snores. Months after she stopped waking her husband to hear better, she still stayed awake to listen.

Amy had been riding just outside the house. Mallory had only turned around for a moment. She'd gone to get the wrench to take off the training wheels. Amy had finally decided she was ready to try riding without them.

Mallory stopped swinging when the moth grew as large as a grapefruit. Its fluttering wings pushed riffles of air toward her face. Her skin prickled. The insect developed black and yellow stripes, and a stinger, and an insistent buzz.

Her mouth opened, silent and frozen.

The bee—it was definitely a bee now—kept growing. Its wings pumped. The window rattled in its frame.

She wanted to whisper to her husband, she wanted to wake him up, she wanted—

The bee, now fat as a watermelon, extended its spindly legs and picked her up. It lifted Mallory from the floor, its tiny claws hooking into her nightgown. With a thrust, it carried her toward the window. She was still too shocked to scream as it dragged her over the windowsill and launched into the night air.

The bee latched on to her nightgown with all six legs, suspending her parallel to the ground like a hang glider. Mallory wriggled in the giant insect's grip until it let go with one leg, swinging her off-kilter over rooftops and trees. She held still, and the bee grabbed the loose end of her nightgown once again.

The bee flew across the neighborhood and into the fields. Mallory dangled below it, shuddering in the cold and shielding her eyes from the rush of wind in her face. Moon-silvered grass and trees flowed below her. Hills rolled up toward her and down again, until they finally reached the coast.

They flew out over the ocean. Mallory looked down over chopping peaks of white froth against inky black water. She felt a jolt and her stomach flew toward her mouth. She was falling. The bee had released her, all six legs at once.

Mallory slammed through the surface of the water, a rag doll thrown through a plate glass window. Icy seawater needled her skin; her nose and mouth filled with brine. She flailed against the waves and swallowed another mouthful of ocean. Her stiff limbs chopped through the surf, which gathered itself and pushed back. She couldn't stay up.

Later (she would never know how long it had actually been) Mallory awoke to something prodding her shoulder. She didn't want to open her eyes. She was warm and dry, and was lying on her side in what felt like sand. Something shook her shoulder again.

A little girl's voice whispered, "Momma?"

Mallory's eyes sprang open to reveal a blurry, sideways image of a little girl squatting next to her. Recognition shot through her body like lightning. She raised her head and blinked.

Amy?

"Uh-oh, Momma," laughed Amy. "Watch out for your horn, you almost got me."

Amy? Baby? Mallory struggled to sit up, her four hooves pawing at sand and air. Her daughter backed away from the flying sand, giggling and brushing off her dress.

Mallory looked down at her body. She was a white horse.

Amy reached toward her again. Mallory's eyes followed her daughter's fingers to the tip of the golden, spiraled horn sprouting from Mallory's forehead. Her vision blurred, this time with tears, as her daughter drew closer. She closed her eyes while Amy carefully stroked her cheeks. Her heart swelled when Amy slid her arms around her neck. She breathed in her baby's sweet warmth, turning her long neck to pull her daughter even closer.

"I missed you, Momma."

Mallory tried to answer, but her reply came out as a whinny. She grunted a couple of times in frustration.

"It doesn't matter, Momma. I still love you."

Mallory nuzzled her daughter.

She and Amy explore the island every day now. They eat juicy red fruits and coconuts that Mallory cracks open with her hooves. She speared a fish with her horn once, but Amy was too squeamish about gutting it, so that was that.

Mallory has lost track of how long she's been gone. Her husband must have filed a missing person report; there must still be a search. Once in a while they hear an airplane and run, giggling and neighing, into the trees to hide until it passes.

Eventually, she knows, there will be a funeral. Her husband will move on. The moth will return to their bedroom in the form of another woman. Perhaps the moth will lay her eggs next summer and bear him dozens of beautiful children. That wouldn't bother Mallory; she's with Amy. She'll see her grow up. Or maybe, on this island, she won't grow up at all.

Mallory can hardly wait to find out.

Tara Campbell

We Are Twenty-Six

Marko's teeth swayed. They twisted and rocked and eased themselves out of his gums while he, heavy with that evening's vodka, grunted and snored in his bed.

On nights when Marko gagged and wheezed in the grips of drink, his teeth longed for their mothers, the baby teeth that had come before them, the first ones to work their way into and out of young Marko's mouth. The little mothers lived together in the small, plastic box in which the tooth fairy had collected them, and which Marko's parents gave to him long after he had stopped believing in the legend of the tooth fairy.

And so that night, as a much older Marko slept, his teeth tumbled out of his mouth. Twenty-six canines, incisors and molars, children of tiny enamel mothers, loosened themselves from his gums and tip-tap-tapped across the floor to the shelves where their forebears now lived. The teeth hopped up the shelves like fleas until they reached the top, where the clear plastic box, now yellowed and filmy, held their brittle little mothers. Their nocturnal adventures always began with these visits: a gentle rap on cloudy plastic, followed by tinkling embraces and enquiries after health.

Because Marko's tooth fairy hadn't been especially diligent, and because one or two of his baby teeth had been swallowed or otherwise lost before collection, and because Marko himself hadn't been exceptionally careful with the box since it had been handed over, not every one of his grown up teeth had its own enamel mother to visit. But all of the teeth were lonesome for a little sliver of a mother, even Marko's wisdom teeth, who had no real mothers to begin with. Fortunately, the mothers had long since forgotten which spot they had occupied, so it didn't really matter. They loved all of Marko's teeth as their own, even the two wisdom teeth who were too severely impacted to ever wiggle out, and had to content themselves with second-hand greetings and kisses upon the return of their siblings.

On this evening, as always, the mothers tut-tutted over Marko's slovenly care of their children. The sibling teeth knew they were stained and full of chips and holes, but could do nothing about it. The mothers would sometimes cry over the three that had been pulled at the dentist's office or the one that had been lost to a barroom brawl; Marko had not thought to bring any of them home.

"He is so inconsiderate," the delicate mothers would complain. "They could have stayed here with us; you could have visited one another here on the shelf."

"Now, now, little mothers," they would answer. "You know we can do nothing about Marko's dereliction, or his thoughtlessness about family reunions."

"Well, you must think of a way to get his attention," the mothers would say.

But the siblings knew where making a fuss could get them—namely in the grip of a dentist's pliers or forgotten on the floor of a bar to be swept into the gutter. And because they knew they could do nothing, they grew impatient of their mothers' mourning. They always took care to leave their mothers before they became too curt with their replies. They assured their brittle little elders not to worry, they would think of something.

The siblings would gently close the yellowed plastic lid then knock and shimmy back down the shelves, pausing to check on Marko. If his breathing was light, they would sneak back in through his parted lips and ease themselves back into his gums.

But if, as they hoped, his breathing was still a raucous, thundering snore, they would tip-tip-tap in a line across the floor, up onto his chair, his desk, and out through his cracked-open window into the night.

This was one of those nights.

They loved to visit the alleys of the town and watch the men play cards and dice—especially dice. The bright white cubes would clack on the ground again and again, and restless men would scoop them up and cradle them like hope, like lovers, breathe on them like babies, speak to them like brothers, "rattle them bones" and throw them out like prayers on the wind.

The teeth were desperate to be part of this magic, to be squeezed, whispered to and hoped for. They would come to the alley as often as they could to watch the men playing their fortunes. Marko would never visit these alleys. He didn't believe in the capricious gambling away of one's future. He believed in the slow, methodical drinking away of it, the comfortable, steady diminishment of one's horizons.

Not so his teeth. They remembered how it felt to flash and shine. Marko had once been young and believed himself dashing, and indeed had often been able to convince others of the same. But somewhere along the way he'd lost track of what his teeth were for, what spark and life were for. Gradually he closed up his face and his heart, pounding back disappointment at the doors that would not open, the women who would not say yes, the barkeeps who stopped donating round after round. Lackluster prospects and unwilling conquests piled up, along with parental disappointment, until Marko eventually learned to drink, work and love within his means, without hope or illusion of more.

His teeth, however, still believed in more. They harbored memories of gleaming when he laughed. They remembered flicking tongues and slick sweat and holding on to sweet, firm flesh. Now there was nothing more than beer and vodka, bread and cigarettes and bile. And why should that be enough? Although they didn't realize it at the time, this was the question they asked themselves that night when they tumbled off the windowsill, slid down the railing, and rattled over the cobblestones into the alley and up to the men.

"Use *us*!" they cried, rolling and jumping. "Scoop us up, breathe on us, speak to us, pray to us, plead with us, trust in us! *Use* us!"

But the men fled, scattering cards, dice, money. The teeth gave chase through fluttering bills and jangling coins, but their clip-clop hopping was no match for legs made long by fear. The teeth gave up, turning instead into another alley filled with the shouts and grunts and laughter of more men, the tap tap tap of spotted dice clattering on the ground.

"Use *us*!" they cried again. "We know all about love and hope and chance and despair. *Use* us!"

But these men, too, were afraid. They bolted out of the alley, abandoning their games, and the teeth knew more about despair than ever before.

"We've lost our edge," moaned an incisor.

"I can't see a way forward," said Marko's remaining eyetooth. "We can't continue this life."

A molar clattered for attention. "I am not a wisdom tooth, but I live next to one. Gather up these dice and follow me."

The teeth knocked against the cool, white cubes in the alley, corralling the dice amongst them and tumbling them down the street. The teeth whispered amongst themselves, pushing their spotted prizes out of cracks and ruts along the way. They lost one die down a grate, but managed to rattle the rest back to the first alley they'd visited that evening.

The molar tapped itself against the scattered cubes the previous group had left behind. "We'll need these too." They departed with their enlarged collection and picked up a few more dice at yet another game they interrupted.

A bird wheedled. The night began to lose its black.

"It's time," said the molar.

The teeth formed a circle and pushed the dice between them, careful not to lose any more. They clicked over tram tracks, tumbled around storm drains and clattered past cigarette butts. They spooked cats and tappety-tapped around rats with their spotted herd, all the way to Marko's door.

"What now?" asked an incisor. "We can't get them inside."

"We can't do *everything* for Marko," the molar replied.

"But we don't have enough," argued the eyetooth. "We are—" It clacked itself against its neighbors to count. "We are twenty-six. We haven't collected *half* enough."

"These will have to do," said the molar. They bumped and knocked the dice into a pile on the front stoop. "Marko will decide what to do next."

The molar hopped up the railing to the cracked-open window. The rest of the teeth followed. They rested on the windowsill and watched Marko roll over in his sleep.

"He'll wake soon," said the incisor.

The teeth turned to face the bookshelf that held the box of their tiny, frail mothers.

Marko snorted and wheezed.

"Goodbye little mothers," whispered the teeth. They leapt off the windowsill, clattered down the railing, and hopped down the street, tip-tap-tapping into the dawn.

Love

&

Consequences

RENDEZVOUS
at hillo like
white elephants

I wait for you in this heat-stained
              blurry-vision place,
fingers tracing my feathered lips,
thinking of the Anis del Toro
and how it would sting.

I wait for you to come,
feeling your parchment hands in the wind,
hot currents pressing against my skin,
opening my mouth to your arid tongue.
I breathe in your sand
as it scatters around me,
I lie down and breathe in your sand,
waiting as you come.

Tara Campbell

Chatroom

Cupping the surrogate curve of a mouse,
fingertips tracing the keyboard instead,
electric elation flows into the house
as she types warm returns to caresses just read.

The Grape

I could have been immaculate,
glowing under golden light,
pearled with condensation
on a burnished copper platter
with a goblet of magenta wine.

He might have made me flawless,
still fresh on a curling green vine
taut with rosy sweetness
just above the farmer's outstretched hand.

He could have painted the perfect grape;
yet he browned in my bruise,
ochered my stem,
and used his entire palette to make me sublime:
purple, plump and shining,
blemished and beautiful and whole,
held aloft by cinnamon finger and thumb,
moving toward the parted cocoa lips
of a hungry lover's mouth.

How long have I had these flowers?

Petals flung brazenly wide,
pistil and stamen erect, waiting for winged satisfaction,
aching for its buzz and thrumming, yearning for its tiptoe hum,
craving its caressing legs, their vicarious union,
with supple tension, anticipating insect-quick agility,
waiting, outstretched a n d o u t s t r e t c h e d .

So how long have I had these flowers of yours?
They've started jerking off onto my desk,
their earthy, orangey semen floating down,
filtering through the grating of my clock
to coat its inner wires with indiscretion,
fouling accuracy with lurid chalk.

And we,
       who time our kisses
       make appointments to hold hands
       and schedule interludes of trust,
squint into our digital sun:

12:00   * * *   12:00   * * *   12:00   * * *   12:00   * * *   12:00

You pull me closer, your hands on my hips.
I breathe in lilies
and taste honey on your lips.

The Real Stuff

I was headin out to feed the cows when I heard a zinnia ask, "You got a minute?"

I shoulda known. When a flower asks you if you got a minute, it's gonna take more'n a minute.

But I didn't think nothin of it at the time. I looked down and all I saw was a few a my wife's pink zinnias stragglin up from a dusty patch a dirt. Their heads was all turned in my direction, so I didn't know at first which one had spoke to me.

"Excuse me?" I asked.

The one in the middle kinda nodded and said, "You got a cup a water or somethin? We're pretty thirsty down here."

I looked around to see who else that zinnia mighta been talkin to, but I don't know why I did that. It was just me and my bony ol' cows out there. Wasn't that fulla people around here before the war, and now… I guess it's just as well, cause we couldn't feed that many folks now anyhow. Can't hardly even feed that many cows. Not much grass since the fallout. Don't get me wrong, we were far enough away from the bombs so that things ain't glowin around here. Still, some things talk now that didn't useta, like some of the plants and birds. And then some things don't really talk anymore that DID useta, like Lizzie and Sarah, my wife and daughter.

But anyhow, these here flowers were askin for some water. The weather changed, see? Don't rain much anymore, so we pipe most of our water in. So I said, "Sorry, flowers, but I don't got a whole lot a water to spare." And they said, "It's all right, farmer, we don't need the good stuff. Any ol' water'll do."

They meant the well water, a'course. Accordin to the tests, it ain't ready for us to drink yet. Shame really, looks so pretty and cool, but we can't touch it. We don't use it for the cows, mind you, so our milk is still good. And they don't get that much grass, like I said, mostly feed from up North; so we're still within legal radiation limits for milk.

So these zinnias—well, I started to feel a little sorry for 'em, just barely ekin out a life in that dusty ol' patch a dirt. We ain't suppose to go near the well, really; I got it fenced off. But I thought, what the hell, ain't nobody else to talk to out here, so I put on my gloves and went ahead and got 'em a bucket-full a water.

And Lord have mercy, what a joyful noise they made. They were so happy they sang. It was this high-pitch, tinklin music, like Tinkerbell, you know? Like a little ol' fairy opera with tiny little flutes or somethin. Their little stalks started swayin back and forth with the music. And the color—I coulda swore that washed out pink color was gettin darker and richer by the minute. I can't describe it near as nice as it was. I could hear my poor cows havin a fit waitin for me, but I didn't want to leave. I musta stood there a good half hour listenin to 'em and watchin 'em sway and get pinker and pinker. It sure was beautiful. By the time I got to the barn, I almost thought the cows were lookin at me mean. Since the fallout, you never know what's gonna start eyein you back like it knows somethin.

Anyway, those zinnias perked up right nice with that water. Every time I went by 'em they waved and said, "Thank you, farmer!" That little corner started smellin real nice. Not real strong and flowery, but still, somethin green and growin gives off a nice, fresh-like smell, don't it? Reminded me of when Lizzie kept all her flowers—zinnias for the butterflies, she would say, hollyhocks for the honey-bees, marigolds for the ladybugs. Mostly all gone now, flowers and critters both.

But these little zinnias, these little scrappers survived somehow, all those years. They were all that was left. I don't know what finally made 'em speak. I guess they just got tired a waitin for Lizzie to come water 'em again, so they started askin me. It wasn't a big chore, and they were awful polite about it. They'd just say, "Hey, farmer, we could use a drop when you get a chance." Real nice-like, not bossy or nothin. So I started goin to the well 'bout once a week or so, give 'em a drink, dust 'em off a little. Get that little breath a somethin good growin, you know?

Got to so I could tell when they needed it. They didn't even have to ask. If I noticed some of the leaves were a little droopy-like, I'd just put on my gloves and head on out to the well.

Sometimes we'd have a little conversation, about the weather, how the cows were doin—though them zinnias didn't really want them cows to get so close, if you know what I mean. I'd set there and reminisce with them flowers about how things useta be, before the war. Sometimes Lizzie and Sarah would come out to take a look at 'em too. I think it pained my wife a little, seein 'em. Kinda reminded her of everything she lost, so she didn't come out a whole lot. And Sarah didn't like the idea of me dippin into that ol' well, but I told her I was bein careful.

I guess I shoulda known, though, those gloves weren't worth a lick against the water; the radiation. I was real careful not to splash any on me, but the gloves—and my hands… In the back a my mind I knew, knew to get them gloves off quick and leave 'em outside, but I guess I wasn't quick enough.

Now seems half the things I touch start talkin. Near as I can figure, it's not things like my feed bucket or a book or a spoon that start gabbin; it's living things like grass and plants and animals that start to talk. I swat a fly, I have to hear it choke out its last will and testament. Was tryin to breed a new strain a corn, but it sasses you back so bad now, I won't be able to sell it to nobody. Have to use a knife and fork to eat a apple—you try eatin somethin that's pleadin for its life.

Even my cows are talkin now, tellin me when they're ready to be milked, if one of 'em has a hoofache, who stole whose allotment a feed. Wishin they had more variety in the trough. Well, that bellyachin stopped when I told 'em what used to show up in cow feed before the war.

Turns out ain't hardly nothin worth listenin to 'cept the zinnias. I can mostly tune all the other talk out, but the gals have a harder time of it. This much noise, seems Lizzie and Sarah got even less to say now than before. But I suppose I didn't think on it that much, 'cause the zinnias were just gettin more and more interesting to listen to. Visiting with 'em got to be a reg'lar part a my day, kinda like my reward after gettin my chores done.

Anyhow, after a while I noticed my hands were itchin and burnin a little. I tried Epsom salts and all kindsa lotions, but even the bag balm didn't help. So I finally went to the doctor. She checked me out, didn't like what she saw. Turns out, ain't just my hands by now. She'll try as best she can, she said, but she don't think there's much can be done. I could keep goin in for treatments or just go home and enjoy my land. Least that much is up to me.

So I keep on tendin to the cows and waterin the zinnias. Had been thinkin about gettin some pigs, but that's Lizzie's say-so now. She and Sarah, they act like they're mad at the flowers, don't come out to visit 'em anymore. 'Course really they're mad at me. My gals don't understand why I did it, why I started lookin after them zinnias, or why I still do it. I wish Lizzie and Sarah would just come out and give 'em another chance. Watch 'em grow, listen to their beautiful music.

They're all connected, you know, the flowers. They all talk. You just need to get past the small talk and find out how deep their roots go, what they're hearin from the dirt, how the other plants around the county are doin. These here zinnias know what the rains are like over the pass and how much sun they're gettin up north. They know how much poison is still left in the ground, what clean air useta smell like—and how much longer we're all gonna have to wait to smell it again. Tendin to these flowers is the only way to know what's really goin on in the world.

I told the zinnias I might not be around to water 'em forever. They wanted to know why, but... Well, I didn't say nothin. It would just kill 'em, and there ain't no need for everything to go to waste. But sooner or later someone else is gonna have to start lookin after 'em. I gotta find someone for 'em soon; someone who wants to hear the good stuff, the real stuff, even if it don't last forever.

Wasted Wishes

His eyes always look so tired now. He seems too young to have eyes that weary; but then, I have no idea how old he really is.

He tells me tales of long ago, of his life among pharaohs and kings. If this is true, I ask, then how did he wind up here, telling his stories in an apartment on the Upper East Side? Sometimes he'll say he doesn't know; that his bottle changed hands too many times to count.

Sometimes he'll just sigh.

We met at a party at a loft in Chelsea. I didn't know whose. He didn't know either. I was impulsive, a closet radical with a job in banking. He was—still is—beautiful. We spent the weekend at my place, rolling around in bed until noon, floating out into a soft-focus world for coffee, ordering dinner in before plunging back into bed.

Weekends stretched into weeks. When we parted ways in the morning he would sling his leather messenger bag over his shoulder like an adventurer heading out into the jungle. Almost every night he would appear at my door with a flower or some small gift tucked into the soft, brown folds of his satchel. He never mentioned where he went on the few nights I didn't see him, and I didn't ask. A current of mystery flowed around him. Enchantment lifted and whirled like a delicate veil, fluttering onto my shoulders and winding around me through our first happy months together.

At night he would stroke my hair and offer me three wishes.

Wish number one: love me, I'd say.

Granted, he'd answer. And your second wish?

I'll wait, I would tell him. I'll wish for something special.

He told me fantastic stories of his life: his childhood in Mesopotamia, the intrigues of the court at Versailles, passage across the Atlantic and, finally, meeting me. He said I was now part of his legend. The mysterious veil fluttered around me again, as light and soft as the wraps of renaissance angels.

I don't remember what our first fight was about: the toothpaste cap, the dishes, something banal and inevitable. That first time, he was gone for a week, returning with flowers and apologies and promises never to leave again. He told me my genie had returned.

But the shadow of the everyday crept toward us, lurking under takeout cartons and piles of laundry. He stayed away longer—two weeks, three weeks, a month—coming back again as though nothing had happened. The last time he disappeared and returned, he told me to make a wish.

I wish you would take a shower, I said.

That's not a real wish, he laughed. But I will comply.

As soon as I heard the water, I opened his messenger bag. I'd had enough mystery. There, with his wallet and phone, I saw a pouch of purple velvet. Its weight surprised me as I lifted it out and loosened the drawstring. I pulled out a small, crude bottle, unevenly blown, with a stopper that only almost fit. The glass was thick and cloudy, stained brown with dirt and age. I jiggled the bottle—nothing. I slowly lifted out the stopper and peered inside—nothing. I turned the bottle around in my hand, wondering what it meant.

The shower went silent. I kept the stopper in my fist and put the rest back into his bag. I didn't know what I wanted with it, what I thought it would do. I just wanted something to change. I wanted a normal life, where people didn't act like genies and disappear for weeks at a time.

I put the stopper somewhere safe, then took it to work to be sure he wouldn't find it. I stared at it every day.

He stayed. Days became weeks, studded with the petty indignities of daily life, and still he stayed.

I buried the stopper in the back of a desk drawer, but I couldn't forget it was there.

Weeks became months, and still he stayed. And his bag never left his sight.

The stopper was a continual, invisible distraction. I could never admit I'd taken it, but hiding it was daily betrayal. One day I finally dug to the back of my drawer, hoping it had somehow disappeared. I wanted it to have burned a hole in my desk and melted through the floor, perhaps found its way back to its bottle, no questions asked. But it was still there.

I took the stopper out and examined it, waiting for it to vanish before my eyes. With my foot, I nudged the trash bin out from under my desk. I held my hand over the bin and looked away, giving the ancient piece of glass one last chance to disappear. I allowed a ringing phone to distract me; I let the stopper fall out of my hand.

And still he stayed. Months became seasons, piling up like dirty dishes. Years oozed on like toothpaste from a crumpled, capless tube. And as we reigned over an empire of laundry and bills, the next ten years crept by behind our backs.

Sometimes, now, I tell him I want to make a wish.

Wish number two, I'll say, never leave me.

That was a wasted wish, he'll say. You know I can't go.

Sometimes, now, I wish for that mysterious, diaphanous veil; to feel its airy silk wrapped around me once again. But that's the one thing he can't conjure up anymore, and there's really nothing else left to wish for.

The Collector

The mermaid wriggled up toward the surface of her lake, eyes fixed on a silver object floating above her. She hovered below the shiny cylinder and plucked it down from its perch between water and air. It was a beer can, dented but still closed. She put it in her plastic shopping bag and dove all the way down to the murky bottom of the lake.

She glided over the bed of silt below, careful not to cloud her vision by stirring up sludge. A dull glint of metal inside a flowing tangle of grasses caught her eye. She pulled at the weeds and extracted a knife. It was a pocketknife this time, smaller than the switchblade she'd found before. Perhaps easier to handle. Triton had been so upset when she'd cut herself slicing water grasses— but not upset enough to move her out of this lake he'd put her in. He was like that, concerned enough to keep her away from all the Mrs. Tritons, but not enough to marry her. He said he'd already hit his wife limit at 5,000. She'd never known of a god with a wife limit, or any other limit for that matter. She folded the pocketknife and slipped it into her bag.

A slight change in current caught her attention. She listened to the water, picking up tiny vibrations that seemed to be coming from the far shore. Lake weed floated and bowed while young carp chased each other around her waist. The vibrations stopped, then started again. The mermaid waved the fish away and went to investigate, the pocketknife and can of beer bumping against her flank as she swam. It took her several minutes, swimming fast, to reach the other end. Triton had wanted her to be comfortable, choosing a lake deep and wide enough for her to swim, play and receive his visits without being discovered.

The water shuddered again. She stopped behind a thick clutch of reeds and put a hand to the bottom of the lake. The heft and timing of the thumping felt like it was coming from grown humans, heavy ones. Probably men. After several minutes the thumping stopped. Quiet. Then came the worm, impaled on a hook.

Breakfast.

The mermaid waited for the hook to sink. She took it gingerly by the eye, slid the worm off, and popped it into her mouth. Then she gave the line a good tug, yanking her hand away as the metal barb shot upward.

She scanned the water for a second hook. There was always a second one. A moment later she found it and ate the second worm. By then, the first hook had reappeared with fresh bait, which she shared with one of the carp that had begun to join her. She batted the fish away from the hooks, as much to get

Circe's Bicycle

first dibs as to keep the fish from getting snagged. The carp were the closest thing she had to company in the lake.

The fishermen fed a few more worms into the lake before giving up. The mermaid remained absolutely still, still enough to hear muffled talking and laughter filter through the water. With a rush of adrenaline, she let herself flirt with the surface, allowing the tip of her tail to flash above water for seconds at a time. Triton had warned her not to let anyone see her. With all the thought he had put into the shape of her lake and its places to hide, she wondered how he could have forgotten the most important variable: curiosity. That "What-Would-Happen-If?" impulse that neither humankind nor mermankind could resist. This was, it occurred to her, a rather large factor not to have considered; especially since it was something she and Triton shared—and was what had eventually landed her in this lake.

The tingle of imminent danger faded when she heard the men thump to their vehicle and drive away. As the vibrations waned, she swam over to her secluded spot on the other side of the lake, beer can in tow. She kept going past the point where the tips of the weeping willow brushed the top of the water. Once behind the curtain of greenery, she broke the surface and wriggled up onto her favorite rock.

She pulled the can of beer out and opened it, taking a first, long drink. Carp circled her rock and she alternated sipping from the can and pouring beer shots into the lake for the fish. She couldn't tell what they were thinking, really, but she hoped they could share in her sunny, happy stupor.

After downing the rest of the beer, she slipped back into the lake, heading for her stash of cigarettes. She pulled herself partway out of the water near a small cave-cache, shaking droplets from her fingers before pulling the grass overhang aside. She grabbed one of the cigarettes she'd skimmed off the surface of the lake and left there to dry. Sticking the crumpled butt into her mouth, she flipped open a small, mangled matchbook she'd found on the shore. Empty! She ripped the cigarette out of her mouth and threw it back into the cache, flopping onto her back and crossing her arms.

As intent as she was on brooding, her concentration was broken by a *click*. Then another one.

She looked out from the shadows behind the weeping willow and saw the back of a boy crouching by the shore. Children often caught her by surprise. Unless they were running, she never felt them coming.

The mermaid wanted to know what the boy was doing, but would have to get closer to see. She slipped into the lake and glided closer, then surfaced only up to the eyes. The boy was still too engrossed in what he was doing to notice her. She inched out from behind the curtain of willow branches, eyes above the water, angling to observe him from the side.

Her heartbeat quickened when she finally saw what he was looking at. It was one of those little rockets, the kind children put in a bottle and light and run. She never got tired of these tiny fireworks, with their sense of danger in miniature. Eyes glued to the rocket, she held her breath, anticipating the crackle of the fuse, the *whoosh* of flight, the *pop!* in the air.

She wouldn't mind having the lighter either. But it didn't seem to work—or was he just not using it correctly? She heard *click* and *click* and *click*, but the fuse wouldn't light. Then the clicking stopped. She looked up and met the boy's eyes.

She twisted downward in a frenzied dive, knowing it was too late. The boy's face peered over the edge of the lake, looming above her through the stream of bubbles she had created. She kept telling Triton this lake was too small; that too many children came here to play. That this was all his fault.

She looked up again and saw the shadow of the boy's head above her. She imagined him on his hands and knees, leaning out over the water, craning his neck to catch another glimpse of her, teetering uncertainly over the water.

That evening the mermaid sat on her favorite rock, smoking a stubby cigarette. She watched the carp slide past one another in the water, knowing she had only one or two more days of peace before the men would come to look for the boy.

One of the carp jumped out of the water onto her rock. It lay still, its mouth opening and closing, gaping again and again as it watched her.

"I know, I'm sorry," she said, and nudged the fish back into the water with the tip of her tail. Soon the men would come to search the shore, then dredge the lake—and now she had one more carp to keep out of harm's way when they got there.

I Remember

My family howls across midnight air. Their cries bound over boulders and twist around trees to lift the hair on the back of my neck. I howl in return, an inadequate croak to their crooning, rich and clear as copper bells. I remember the blood of our last hunt on the forest floor, slick on night-blacked leaves.

I turn my head to pinpoint their location (my ears do not swivel anymore) and stumble through the underbrush, my two feet crashing where four paws used to glide. Long after they have scented me, I smell them, the pungent musk of their fur, the stink of their breath slipping out between jagged teeth and lolling tongues.

I enter a moon-drenched clearing and the howling stops. My mother and sister pad out from the inky treeline into the open glade. I move toward them and they yip in anticipation. I yelp back, putting away the feeling of imitation, of mocking. This is as well as I can do after all these months.

They want to know everything immediately, of course, but they will wait until we're with the rest of the pack. With whines and yips and growls I will tell them everything that has happened since I undertook the painful transformation to search for my father. I will tell them that I located him, that he now lives behind bars in a dusty, concrete forest where his kills are tossed to him already cold and dead.

Every month I return to tell the pack about the special clothing I wear and the things I say to get closer to my father. I tell them how words twist and curl like worms on my stumpy human tongue before falling from my mouth. I must demonstrate my expertise, prove that I am skilled enough to be my father's keeper. He has only a dim sense of who I am in my current form, yet the other humans marvel at our connection. They will be even more surprised one day when they find both of us gone.

I cannot blame my father for not knowing me. He did not witness my transition. He did not whine with me as I gobbled down the kind old woman's special roots, or pace with me as I followed her steps. He did not pant and circle while she held my body and watched it quake with fracture, bleed, break itself apart and knit itself back together into something weak and naked and new.

The pack watched me transform, keening their misery at my pain and bellowing gratitude when I wobbled to a stand, on two legs, to track my father. When I bring him back home, the spell will reverse. But every month when I return, they ask more questions. Things I've already told them. They do not remember, and lately when I talk to them, I become confused myself.

The new pups in the pack do not know my scent.

In the clearing, my mother and sister prowl from side to side on eager paws. Their noses lift to meet invisible currents, and moonlight burnishes their dull grey coats to glistening silver. They turn away from me and slip back into the forest, where the rest of the pack waits. They look back at me, twin sparks of their eyes dancing in the gloom. Their eyes shimmer in the blackness, gleaming like drops of blood on night-blacked leaves. Someday, when even they begin to forget me, their teeth will flash brighter still.

Credits

"Freedom Bras" originally published in *District Lit*, March 2017

"When Peanut Butter Baby Ruled the World" originally published in *Zetetic: A Record of Unusual Inquiry*, July 2016

"Where the Words Go" originally published in *SmokeLong Quarterly*, April 2017

"Captain John's Passage" originally published in *Helios Quarterly*, July 2016

"Circe's Bicycle" originally published in *Defenestrationism Short Story Challenge*, July 2016

"We Are Twenty-Six" originally published in *The Indianola Review*, June 2016

"Rendezvous at hills like white elephants" originally published in *Peregrine Journal*, May 2016

"Chatroom" originally published in *Mt. Pleasant Poetry Anthology*, May 2016

"How long have I had these flowers?" originally published in *The London Journal of Fiction*, November 2015

"The Real Stuff" originally published in *T. Gene Davis's Speculative Blog*, March 2014; republished in *Strange Changes* (Whortleberry Press), January 2016

"Wasted Wishes" originally published in *The Masters Review*, June 2014

"The Collector" originally published in *Latchkey Tales, Elementals: Children of Water*, July 2014

Tara Campbell (www.taracampbell.com) is the recipient of the following awards from the DC Commission on the Arts and Humanities: the Larry Neal Writers' Award in fiction, the Mayor's Arts Award for Outstanding New Artist, and a 2018 Arts and Humanities Fellowship. She's a fiction editor at *Barrelhouse*, an MFA candidate at American University, and a 2017 Kimbilio Fellow. Prior publication credits include *SmokeLong Quarterly*, *Masters Review*, *b(OINK)*, *Booth*, *Spelk*, *Litbreak*, and *Queen Mob's Teahouse*. Her debut novel, *TreeVolution*, was published in 2016.

www.ingramcontent.com/pod-product-compliance
Lightning Source LLC
LaVergne TN
LVHW051430080426
835508LV00022B/3332